ARGENTINA TRAVEL GUIDE

2023

A Comprehensive Guide to Exploring the Heart of South America, the Amazing Culture, Cuisine & Landscapes

Mitchell H Cole

COPYRIGHT

CONTENTS

WELCOME TO ARGENTINA

I was thrilled to finally have the opportunity to go to Argentina since I had always wanted to. I arrived in Buenos Aires via plane and fell in love with its distinctive charm and vigor right away. I toured the city for a few days, soaking in the sights and sounds and savoring the delectable cuisine. I spent a few days in the capital before leaving to go the rest of the way.

My adventure began in the breathtaking Lake District, where I stayed in a little mountain village with a lake view. My days were spent trekking in the nearby mountains, soaking in the amazing views, and unwinding by the lakeshore. I also went to the adjacent towns, where I had the chance to experience the local food, learn about the culture, and tour the lively marketplaces.

I next traveled to Cordoba, the bustling and chaotic capital of the nation. I spent a few days touring the city, admiring the colonial architecture, going to a lot of museums and art galleries, and, of course, eating at lots of fantastic restaurants and drinking in lots of great pubs. I also went exploring the nearby countryside, where I had a chance to learn about the customs and culture of the area firsthand. I eventually traveled to the country's north, where I took in the breathtaking Iguazu Falls. I admired the magnificent falls for a whole day while also visiting the nearby forests. I was able to interact closely with the animals when I took a boat excursion down the river.

I will always cherish the amazing experience I had while visiting Argentina. I got to take in the breathtaking surroundings, discover the native way of life, and savor some delectable local food. I can't wait to return and discover more of this wonderful nation.

SECTION ONE

WHY VISIT ARGENTINA

Argentina is a nation rich in culture, history, and stunning scenery. A trip to Argentina is guaranteed to be one to remember, from the energetic capital city of Buenos Aires to the magnificent Andes Mountains.

The Iguazu Falls, the Perito Moreno Glacier, and the El Glaciares National Park are just a few of the top attractions in the nation. Visitors visiting Argentina have the opportunity to learn more about the local culture by seeing local markets, art galleries, and museums.

Argentina is renowned for its deep cultural heritage in addition to its natural beauty. Explore the many cultures of the nation, from the native Mapuche to the offspring of European immigration. Visitors will find a nation rich in culture, from the Pampas' gaucho history to the tango's traditional music.

Another attraction for tourists is the cuisine of Argentina. The diverse delicacies of the nation, like the well-known Argentine steak and the traditional empanadas and locro, are guaranteed to please tourists. Visitors visiting Argentina should also be sure to try some of the greatest wines in the world, which are produced there. For those who like the great outdoors, Argentina is a fantastic location. There are several sports available for travelers to enjoy, like horseback riding in Patagonia and hiking and mountain biking in the Andes. Argentina has plenty to offer everyone, whether they want to unwind on the beach or explore the countryside.

Visitors to Argentina should be sure to set aside some time to unwind. Argentina has rich locations that provide refuge and relaxation, from the busy city to the serene countryside. Argentina offers both romantic getaways and leisurely vacations, so there is something for everyone.

Argentina may be visited for a variety of reasons, but its natural beauty is a main attraction. A trip to Argentina is guaranteed to be one to remember, from the magnificent Andes Mountains to the energetic culture of Buenos Aires. Argentina is certain to have something unique to offer tourists wishing to experience the country's culture, take in its natural beauty, or just unwind and take it all in.

History

Argentina is a nation in South America with a lengthy, diverse, and complicated history. It is a country with a complex political history and a wide variety of cultures and races. Indigenous Mapuche people who lived in what is now Argentina as early as 9,000 BC are the earliest known occupants of the area. The Viceroyalty of the River de la Plata and the Captaincy General of Chile were the two administrative entities that governed the area by the time the Spanish had established a colony on the eastern bank of the Rio de la Plata in the 16th century.

During the Napoleonic Wars, the area proclaimed its independence from Spain and created the United Provinces of the Ro de la Plata at the beginning of the 19th century. Argentina formed one country in 1852 after a period of political unrest and civil conflicts. In the late 19th century, the nation saw a period of economic expansion and prosperity, and by 1914, it had become one of Latin America's richest nations.

Nonetheless, the nation started to endure political unrest at the beginning of the 20th century. In 1930, the military ousted the government and installed a dictatorship under the direction of General Juan Perón. Under Perón's tenure, the nation went through a time of economic expansion and stability, but it also became more authoritarian.

Once the military once again assumed power in the 1950s, a new era of political instability started. Argentina saw many military takeovers, civil wars, and economic crises throughout this time. This phase of unrest persisted until the 1980s when General Leopoldo Galtieri's military rule over the nation brought about severe economic hardship and violations of human rights. The nation started moving toward democracy in the late 1980s and early 1990s, and a new constitution was adopted in 1994. Argentina has since gone through phases of economic expansion, political stability, and heightened social and political freedoms.

Argentina is a dynamic country with a diversified population and a lively culture today. It is one of South America's most economically developed nations and has made significant strides in advancing political and human rights. Argentina has developed into a regional role model for political and economic stability despite its turbulent history.

Weather and Climate

Due to its vastness, Argentina offers a broad variety of climates and weather patterns. Its length from north to south is over 3,500 km (2,175 miles), and its climate varies greatly from the subtropical north to the subpolar south. Temperatures in Argentina's northern region often range from mild to hot and are humid. Summers there are hot and muggy, with highs of up to 35 °C (95 °F). The winters are moderate and mostly dry, with lows that sometimes dip below 8 °C (46 °F). In the north, where thunderstorms are frequent, rainfall is maximum in the summer.

Argentina's center areas have a relatively moderate climate. The summers are scorching and arid, with highs of up to 35 °C (95 °F). The winters are harsh and arid, with lows that may reach -5 °C (23 °F). The amount of rain is less and more erratic than in the north.

Argentina's southern region has substantially colder weather. The summers are moderate and mostly dry, with highs of 25 °C (77 °F). The winters are harsh and damp, with lows as low as -10°C (14°F). Wintertime brings the most rain, and higher altitudes often have snowfall during this time.

Argentina's climate is usually warm, with temperatures seldom dipping below -10°C (14°F) or rising over 35°C (95°F). The nation is vulnerable to extreme weather, especially in the northern and central parts of the country. This includes thunderstorms, hailstorms, and floods. Argentina is renowned for its powerful winds in addition to its diverse climate. The area of southern Patagonia has the greatest winds, with gusts reaching up to 120 km/h (75 mph). Strong winds have the potential to seriously harm crops and infrastructure, as well as sometimes create power outages.

Argentina offers a diverse spectrum of climates and weather patterns, to sum up. Although the south is much cooler, the northern and central parts are often warm and muggy. Throughout the nation, severe weather is frequent, especially in the north and center areas, while high winds are frequent in the south.

People and Culture

A rich and varied culture may be found in Argentina. The culture reflects the population's mixture of European, Native American, and African influences.

Argentina's inhabitants are renowned for being cheerful and hospitable. Argentinians are happy to share their culture and history with tourists and are quite hospitable to them. They are renowned for their enjoyment of cuisine, dancing, and music. A significant component of the culture is music, and the streets are filled with sounds from all over the globe.

Argentina's national soccer team is one of the most successful in the world, and the country has a strong soccer culture. Many people play and watch soccer, and enthusiasm for the sport is evident at the stadiums and on the streets. Argentina's food is likewise quite varied, ranging from classic meals to contemporary fusion cuisine. Argentinians are enthusiastic about their cuisine, and there are many eateries providing cuisine from throughout the globe. Yerba mate, a classic tea-like beverage, is often offered as a side with Argentine cuisine.

In Argentina, where the Roman Catholic Church is the dominant religion, religion is significant. Judaism, Islam, and Protestantism are among the other faiths prevalent in the nation. The Mapuche, Guarani, and Qom are just a few of the Indigenous cultures that may be found in Argentina. These cultures are often represented in art, music, and dance, and there are several festivals held all year long to honor them.

The people and culture of Argentina are a reflection of the stunning and varied landscape of the nation. It is a beautiful destination to come and discover with its lively music, passionate people, and varied food.

Must know (10 things to know before Visiting Argentina)

1. Language: Spanish is the official language of Argentina, so it's a good idea to brush up on your vocabulary before traveling there. While Spanish is widely spoken in large cities and tourist destinations, knowing a little bit of it is still helpful.

2. Money: The Argentine Peso is the country's legal currency (ARS). It is simple to locate currency exchange offices in big cities, thus it is advised to carry both cash and credit cards.

3. Climate: Argentina's climate ranges from subtropical to temperate to dry. The finest seasons to travel are spring and autumn when the weather is pleasant.

4. Security: In general, Argentina is a secure nation, although it's important to follow the standard security

protocols. Keep an eye on your surroundings, don't carry a lot of cash, and steer clear of nighttime alone wandering.

5. Transportation: Buses are the most widely used kind of public transportation across the nation. There are also taxis available, although it's advisable to negotiate a rate before boarding.

6. Cuisine: Don't miss out on sampling some of the regional delicacies; Argentina is renowned for its cattle and wine. Pastas, dulce de leche, and empanadas are a few further popular foods.

7. Wildlife: Guanacos, pumas, and flamingos are just a few of the animals that can be found in Argentina. Alpacas and llamas may also be found in the northern parts of the nation.

8. Tipping: In Argentina, it is traditional to tip, and most restaurants tack on a 10-15% service fee to the bill. You

may give an additional few pesos as a tip if the service was exceptional.

9. Attire: While Argentina's dress code is often informal, it is important to dress up for dinner and other formal events. Bring a couple of dressy clothes for these events.

10. Patience: While Argentines are recognized for their energy and passion, don't be shocked if things take a little longer than usual. Argentina is a country where patience is essential, so take your time and enjoy yourself.

SECTION TWO

EXPLORING ARGENTINA

Exploring Argentina is a fantastic experience that provides a special fusion of adventure, culture, and environment. Argentina has something for everyone, from the cosmopolitan city of Buenos Aires and Mendoza to the spectacular scenery of Patagonia.

Buenos Aires is the ideal location for anyone interested in culture. The city, which is rich in both history and culture, is home to some of South America's top theaters, galleries, and museums. The Latin American Art Museum's galleries, San Telmo's cobblestone alleys, and La Boca's tango lessons are all accessible to visitors.

Argentina is a naturalist's delight. The nation is filled with stunning scenery, from the verdant Iguazu Falls to the snow-capped Andes Mountains. Trekking through the historic woodlands of the Lake District, discovering the glaciers of Patagonia, or unwinding on the Mar del Plata beaches are all options for tourists.

Those who desire adventure won't be let down either. World-class mountain riding, whitewater rafting, and skiing are available in Argentina. Tourists may learn to kitesurf at El Calafate or go up Aconcagua, the tallest mountain in the Americas.

Argentina will undoubtedly have plenty to offer every kind of tourist. The nation is one of the most varied and intriguing travel destinations in South America, with dynamic cities and stunning scenery. Argentina will undoubtedly have everything you're searching for, whether you're seeking adventure, nature, or culture.

Top must-see Attractions (The Ultimate Bucket list)

The Iguazu Falls

The Iguazu Falls, a magnificent waterfall system made up of 275 distinct cascades and drops that span approximately 2 miles, are situated on the border between Argentina and Brazil. From the many paths and viewpoints, visitors may see the splendor of the falls, or they can take a boat trip to the base of the falls.

Buenos Aires

Buenos Aires, the dynamic capital of Argentina, is a city brimming with culture and energy. There is something for everyone in Buenos Aires, from the stunning architecture and cobblestone alleys of the old San Telmo area to the hip restaurants and bars of Palermo.

Perito Moreno Glacier

The Perito Moreno Glacier is a breathtaking natural marvel that can be seen in Argentina's Patagonia area. It's amazing to see the glacier calve regularly. Tourists may stroll along the glacier's edge or take boat trips to come up close to the glacier.

27

Ushuaia

Situated on Argentina's southernmost point, Ushuaia serves as a gateway to Antarctica. The Beagle Channel, magnificent mountains, and majestic glaciers that encircle the city make it a fantastic location for outdoor activities.

El Calafate

A little town with a great personality, El Calafate is situated in Argentina's Patagonian area. The town offers a wide range of outdoor activities in addition to fantastic restaurants, cafés, and pubs. The nearby Perito Moreno Glacier, which is accessible by boat, is another attraction open to visitors.

Mendoza

Mendoza is the wine capital of Argentina and is situated in the foothills of the Andes Mountains. Tourists may ride bicycles across the countryside or explore the region's many wineries and local beverages.

Tierra del Fuego

Located in Argentina's far south, Tierra del Fuego is a breathtakingly gorgeous area of the nation. Travelers may trek the several paths in the region, take a boat across the Magellan Strait, or go on a 4x4 safari to explore the rough terrain.

Salta

Situated in Argentina's north, Salta is a lovely colonial city with a distinctive fusion of cultures and architectural styles. The city's many sights may be explored, local food can be tried, or a train journey down the adjacent Quebrada de Humahuaca can be taken.

Córdoba

This vibrant city in central Argentina is home to a wide variety of cultural traditions. Tourists may walk around the Plaza San Martin or explore the vibrant districts. They can also visit the many churches and cathedrals.

El Chaltén

El Chaltén is a little but picturesque mountain village that may be found in Argentina's Patagonian area. Tourists may take tours of the adjacent glaciers, trek to the stunning Fitz Roy mountain, or explore the beautiful lakes.

Argentinian Highlights

Argentina is a stunning nation with a vibrant culture and a wealth of amazing adventures. There are many options for exploration and adventure, from Patagonia's breathtaking mountains to Argentina's busy capital city of Buenos Aires. These are some of the best Argentina experiences that everyone should add to their bucket list.

Go to Buenos Aires

The busy and colorful capital of Argentina is home to some of South America's greatest nightlife, dining, and museums. Explore the vibrant La Boca neighborhood while strolling through the ancient San Telmo district's cobblestone streets. Or enroll in a tango class at one of the numerous dancing establishments. Whatever you choose to do in Buenos Aires, it will undoubtedly be an amazing experience.

Go to Patagonia

Patagonia is a big area with stunning scenery and amazing fauna. Visit the El Glaciares National Park on a hiking excursion to see the magnificent Perito Moreno Glacier. Instead, go to the continent's southernmost point and see the untamed Tierra del Fuego archipelago. Patagonia is a fantastic region of the globe to visit, whether you go trekking, horseback riding, or kayaking.

Go on a wine tour

Argentina produces some of the world's finest wines. Discover the best vineyards in Argentina by traveling to the Mendoza area. Learn all there is to know about the terroir and the winemaking process by taking a guided tour of the vineyards. Try a couple of the regional wines and bring a few bottles home as mementos.

4. Go to Iguazu Falls, one of the world's most breathtaking natural marvels. The bordering cascading waterfalls between Argentina and Brazil provide breathtaking vistas from both sides. Get up and personal

with the rumbling falls by taking a boat trip. Instead, go on a forest hike and search for unusual creatures.

Drink Mate

Popular across Argentina, mate is a classic South American tea. It is consumed out of a gourd and is prepared from dried yerba mate plant leaves. Discover how to brew the ideal cup of a mate so you may indulge in it when you're traveling.

Visit El Calafate's Glaciers

El Calafate is a little hamlet in southern Argentina. Some of the most beautiful glaciers in the world may be found there. See the Perito Moreno Glacier by boat and get a close-up look at the frozen terrain. Instead, take a hiking excursion across the flawless countryside and take in the breathtaking sights.

Go to Quilmes Ruins

In the northwest of Argentina, Quilmes is a pre-Columbian archaeological site. The 14th-century remains include a confusing network of stone walls and terraces. See the ruins up close and learn about the site's past by taking a guided tour.

Argentina offers a variety of experiences for visitors, no matter what they're searching for. Everyone may find something to explore in this amazing nation, from the energetic metropolitan life of Buenos Aires to the breathtaking scenery of Patagonia.

SECTION THREE

GETTING THERE

Argentina may be reached in a comparatively simple and easy manner. You have a variety of choices for getting around depending on where you are coming from.

By Air

Air travel is a fun and practical way to visit Argentina, which is a beautiful nation. Travelers have a wide range of alternatives for flying because of the nation's many airports. It's crucial to take the airport you'll be landing at into account when booking a trip. Aeroparque Jorge Newbery in Buenos Aires, Ministro Pistarini International Airport in Ezeiza, and El Palomar Airport in Buenos Aires are Argentina's biggest and busiest airports. You may wish to choose one of these airports for the most convenient journey depending on your final destination.

Booking a flight is the next step after selecting an airport. You may book flights to Argentina online, via travel agents, or on direct flights from other nations. Aerolineas Argentinas, American Airlines, Delta Air Lines, British Airways, KLM, and Lufthansa are just a few of the airlines that fly nonstop to Argentina. These airlines often provide outstanding service and costs that are competitive. You must pass immigration and customs when you arrive in Argentina. You must also have a current passport and visa. Remember to correctly and thoroughly complete the immigration paperwork. There may be extra requirements for tourists, such as vaccines or visas, depending on your place of origin.

You may start your adventure in Argentina after clearing customs. Argentina has something for everyone, from the city of Buenos Aires to the stunning Patagonian area in the south. Argentina has both the excitement and the calm vacation you're searching for.

The best method to visit Argentina is via plane, which is a fantastic kind of transportation. Travelers may choose flights that work with their schedule and budget thanks to access to some of the biggest airports in the globe. There are several ways to get to Argentina, whether you choose a direct trip or a connecting flight. After you are there, you may start exploring this lovely nation and all it has to offer.

By Rail

Argentina is a big, varied nation with many distinct attractions, and taking the train is a terrific way to see them all. From Argentina's northern border to its southernmost point, as well as to many of its main towns, travel is accessible thanks to the country's extensive network of railway lines.

Choosing a route is the first step in taking a train to Argentina. Several lines connect the nation's capital, Buenos Aires, with other significant cities, including Mendoza and Cordoba. Other lines run to other nations like Chile and Brazil. It is advisable to do a prior study on rail routes and timetables to choose the optimal path.

Buying tickets is the next step. You may buy tickets at a ticket office at a train station or online via the Argentine Railway website. Check the precise train timetable and route before purchasing tickets since weather or other circumstances often cause schedule modifications. Before purchasing tickets, it's also a good idea to compare rates since they may change based on the day of the week and the kind of tickets selected. It's crucial to keep in mind to pack all required materials and paperwork, including a passport and a valid ID, before taking the train. Travelers should be cautious to verify the prerequisites beforehand since certain lines can additionally need a visa. Also, it's crucial to pack comfortable clothes and travel essentials like books, food, and snacks.

As the voyage progresses, passengers may take in Argentina's breathtaking countryside as they pass through well-known cities and villages. Travelers passing through the nation may see a variety of landscapes, from the Amazon's lush rainforest to the Andes' snow-capped mountains.

Argentina may be explored and its various attractions can be enjoyed best through train travel. It is a terrific way to see the nation without having to worry about lengthy vehicle drives or pricey flights because of its handy lines and pleasant trains. Rail travel is a terrific way to see Argentina in all its beauty and variety, whether you're going to the city or a far-off village.

By Road

A thrilling and adventurous method to travel in Argentina is by car. You can get about by car, bus, or even bicycle. Depending on your schedule, travel preferences, and financial constraints, there are many different ways to go to Argentina by car.

Bus travel is the most economical alternative if you're searching for a means to go to Argentina on the road. It is simple to travel from numerous countries in South America to Argentina by bus thanks to firms like El Rapido, El Expreso, and Andesmar. Depending on where you are going, the trip might take anything from 18 hours to 3 days. Due to the reasonable cost of bus tickets, traveling to Argentina by bus is a preferred method.

Driving is the best option if you want to see the country at your speed. You may either drive your vehicle over the border or hire a car in Argentina. While certain roads in Argentina might be difficult owing to their state, driving is generally not too difficult there. You will need a current international driver's license if you are traveling by car from a nearby nation like Chile or Bolivia.

Last but not least, you might choose to go by bicycle if you're seeking an even more adventurous approach to reaching Argentina. This is a fantastic chance to see some of the more off-the-beaten-path parts of the nation while traveling at a much slower speed. The majority of the nation has riding routes, and there are a lot of bike trips available.

It's a thrilling and distinctive experience to go to Argentina by car. Depending on your travel preferences and budget, several solutions are available. Whether you decide to go by car, bus, or bicycle, you can be sure that the journey will be one to remember.

Getting around

Argentina is a sizable nation with many different modes of transportation. Argentina offers a variety of options to travel the nation, from long-distance buses and trains to short-distance shuttles and rental automobiles.

Bus

Bus travel is the preferred mode of transportation in Argentina. The La Empresa de Transporte national bus system, which connects most major cities, is one of the least expensive means of transportation. The majority of the buses have Internet and air conditioning, and they are cozy and secure.

Train

From Buenos Aires to Bariloche and other locations, the Ferrocarril General Roca, the country's rail network, runs. A range of seating classes, including first-class and economy, are available for purchase at any of the stations by patrons. The trains are a terrific way to view the countryside and are pleasant and clean.

Car lease

Another well-liked method of transportation in Argentina is via car. Airports and the majority of big cities have rental vehicle agencies. Rental companies provide a range of vehicle sizes, and automobiles are usually trustworthy and clean. The driver's age must be at least 21 and the license must be current. It's vital to keep in mind that parts of Argentina's roads could be challenging to handle, so it's better to plan your itinerary.

Shuttles

In Argentina, shuttles are an excellent method to travel. Several towns and cities have shuttle services, which may be booked online or at the closest bus terminal. Generally speaking, shuttles are dependable and clean, and they often provide discounts for large parties or many passengers.

Taxi

Most cities and towns also have taxi services accessible. The cabs are normally trustworthy, and the drivers are kind and accommodating. The fee should be agreed upon before the driver begins the meter since it is depending on the distance traveled. Credit card payments are often accepted.

To sum up, Argentina is a sizable nation with a range of transportation choices. Travelers may easily find a method to see the nation, whether they choose long-distance buses and trains or short-distance shuttles and rental automobiles. Whatever the kind of transportation you use, be careful to plan your trip and be aware of the safety concerns before you go.

SECTION FOUR

HOTELS AND
ACCOMODATIONS

Argentina is a country in South America with a vibrant culture and a variety of tourist destinations, including the magnificent Iguazu Falls and the busy Buenos Aires. Argentina has something for everyone, whether they want to explore the cities, partake in the exciting nightlife, or enjoy the outdoors. Argentina has a vast selection of hotels, bed & breakfasts, and hostels to accommodate any choice or budget.

Hotels in Argentina vary from opulent five-star complexes to straightforward, affordable lodgings. All the amenities that customers might anticipate from a five-star hotel are offered by luxury accommodations, including lavish spas, fine dining, and contemporary comforts. They often reside in large cities like Buenos Aires and Cordoba. There are mid-range hotels in all the main cities that provide pleasant, basic lodging. For tourists seeking more affordable accommodation, budget hotels are a fantastic alternative. These may be found in most cities and towns, and they are typically simple and clean.

Particularly for tourists seeking a more personal experience, bed & breakfasts are a popular lodging option in Argentina. B&Bs are primarily family-run enterprises that are situated in residential areas. They often provide visitors the opportunity to have a home-cooked supper and learn about the local way of life. Another excellent choice for tourists on a budget is hostels. The majority of hostels in Argentina include standard services including communal kitchens, restrooms, and common areas. They are a terrific opportunity to meet other people and learn more about the local way of life since they are often found in busy areas.

Argentina offers a vast variety of lodging alternatives, regardless of the kind of lodging a visitor is seeking. Hostels, hotels, and bed & breakfasts all provide cozy ways to travel across the nation. Argentina provides options for everyone, whether you're seeking an opulent resort or a cheap hostel.

Budget-Friendly Hotels

1. La Casa de los Once Patios - Situated in the center of San Telmo, La Casa de los Once Patios provides affordable lodging in a distinctive environment. It boasts a historical structure with a rooftop terrace, a pool, and 11 patios. The rooms are basic yet pleasant and provide free Wi-Fi. It also provides a free breakfast.

2. Hostel Suites Palermo - Located in the hip Palermo district, Hostel Suites Palermo is an affordable hotel. It provides cozy accommodations with separate bathrooms, a/c, and complimentary WiFi. Also, it contains a pool, a rooftop deck, and a community kitchen.

3. Hotel Piedras Blancas - Situated in the center of Buenos Aires, Hotel Piedras Blancas is a budget-friendly lodging option. It provides cozy lodging with air conditioning and private toilets. It also features a restaurant, a bar, and a pool.

4. Hotel Bellavista - This low-cost hotel is situated in the ancient city of La Boca. It provides cozy lodging with air conditioning and private toilets. In addition, it contains a bar, a restaurant, and a swimming pool.

5. Hotel de la Vina - This budget-friendly hotel is situated in the lovely city of Mendoza. It provides cozy accommodations with separate bathrooms, a/c, and complimentary WiFi. In addition, it contains a bar, a restaurant, and a swimming pool.

6. Hotel Abasto - This budget-friendly hotel is situated in the center of Buenos Aires. It provides cozy accommodations with separate bathrooms, a/c, and complimentary WiFi. There is also a restaurant and Bar

7. Hostel Pucara - Located in Córdoba, Hostel Pucara is a budget-friendly hostel. It provides cozy accommodations with separate bathrooms, a/c, and complimentary WiFi.

8. Hotel San Jorge - Located in the lovely city of San Juan, Hotel San Jorge is a reasonably priced hotel. It provides cozy accommodations with separate bathrooms, a/c, and complimentary WiFi.

9. Hotel Caballito - Located in Buenos Aires, Hotel Caballito is a reasonably priced hotel. It provides cozy lodging with air conditioning and private toilet

10. Hotel Nogaro - This budget-friendly lodging option is situated in the center of Bariloche. It provides cozy lodging with air conditioning and private toilets. In addition, it contains a bar, a restaurant, and a swimming pool.

Bed and Breakfast

1. Casa Sur Art Hotel: This opulent boutique hotel is situated in Buenos Aires' chic Palermo Soho neighborhood. It offers visitors a distinctive fusion of cutting-edge conveniences and classic elegance. The hotel's serene and quiet setting complements its chic and modern architecture. The hotel's services and amenities, which include a rooftop pool, a spa, and a yoga studio, are all accessible to guests. For visitors' enjoyment, Casa Sur Art Hotel also has several eating alternatives, including a restaurant and bar.

2. The Glu Hotel: Located in the center of Buenos Aires's business district. It provides luxurious, contemporary lodging with roomy bedrooms and apartments. From a restaurant and bar to a fitness center and spa, visitors may make use of a variety of facilities. The Glu Hotel also has a rooftop patio and pool where visitors may unwind and enjoy city views.

3. Hotel Madero: Situated in the hip Puerto Madero neighborhood of Buenos Aires, this boutique hotel provides visitors with a tranquil retreat in the middle of the bustling city. The hotel has opulent bedrooms and suites that are both stylish and contemporary. In addition, Hotel Madero offers a variety of services, including a restaurant, bar, fitness center, and spa.

4. The Uxua House Hotel & Spa: Situated in San Telmo's historic quarter, this boutique hotel presents visitors with a distinctive fusion of modern style and traditional Argentine culture. The hotel offers roomy bedrooms and suites as well as a variety of facilities, including a restaurant, bar, rooftop pool, and spa. Also, visitors have access to a variety of activities, including cycling and horseback riding as well as yoga and meditation courses.

5. The Home Hotel: Located in Buenos Aires' hip Palermo Hollywood neighborhood, this boutique hotel offers an exceptional mix of elegance and comfort. The hotel offers a variety of services, including a restaurant,

bar, fitness center, and spa, along with contemporary and elegant bedrooms and suites. Also, visitors have access to a variety of activities, including cycling and horseback riding as well as yoga and meditation courses.

6. The Hotel Boca Juniors: Located in the center of Buenos Aires' business district. With roomy bedrooms and suites, it provides visitors with a distinctive fusion of elegance and comfort. From a restaurant and bar to a fitness center and spa, visitors may make use of a variety of facilities. Moreover, the Hotel Boca Juniors has a rooftop patio and pool where visitors may unwind and enjoy city views.

7. The Legado Mitico Hotel: Situated in Buenos Aires' hip Palermo Soho neighborhood, this boutique hotel offers visitors a distinctive mix of elegance and comfort. The hotel offers a variety of services, including a restaurant, bar, fitness center, and spa, along with contemporary and elegant bedrooms and suites. Also, visitors have access to a variety of activities, including

cycling and horseback riding as well as yoga and meditation courses.

8. La Cantera Boutique Hotel: Located in the center of downtown Buenos Aires, this boutique hotel provides visitors with opulent bedrooms and suites as well as a contemporary and fashionable place to stay. In addition, La Cantera Boutique Hotel offers a variety of services, including a restaurant, bar, fitness center, and spa. Also, visitors have access to a variety of activities, including cycling and horseback riding as well as yoga and meditation courses.

9. Hotel Fierro: This chic boutique hotel is situated in Buenos Aires's Palermo Hollywood neighborhood. It offers visitors a distinctive fusion of cutting-edge conveniences and classic elegance. The hotel offers roomy bedrooms and suites as well as a variety of services, including a restaurant, bar, fitness center, and spa. Also, visitors have access to a variety of activities, including cycling and horseback riding as well as yoga and meditation courses.

10. The Unique Hotel: Located in the center of Buenos Aires' business district. It provides opulent bedrooms and suites with contemporary and fashionable accommodations. In addition, The Unique Hotel offers a variety of services, including a restaurant, bar, fitness center, and spa. Also, visitors have access to a variety of activities, including cycling and horseback riding as well as yoga and meditation courses.

Luxury hotels

1. Alvear Palace Hotel: The Alvear Palace Hotel, a five-star luxury hotel in Buenos Aires, provides the finest in elegance and comfort to all of its visitors. The hotel, which is a member of the Leading Hotels of the World group, offers several facilities and services. The hotel's restaurant, bar, and lounge, as well as its spa and fitness center, are all available to guests. The hotel's rooms and suites are roomy and equipped with contemporary conveniences including flat-screen TVs, air conditioning, and free Wi-Fi.

2. Park Hyatt Mendoza: Situated in the center of Mendoza, the Park Hyatt Mendoza is a chic and contemporary five-star hotel. This opulent hotel provides its visitors with a wide range of facilities, including an outdoor pool, a fitness center, and a selection of eating choices. The hotel's rooms and suites include elegant design and modern conveniences including flat-screen Televisions, air conditioning, and free WiFi.

3. The Vines Resort & Spa: This opulent five-star hotel is situated in the center of Mendoza and provides its visitors with the ultimate luxury and relaxation. The hotel offers several services and facilities, such as an outdoor pool, a fitness center, and a selection of restaurants. The hotel's rooms and suites are tastefully furnished and equipped with flat-screen Televisions, air conditioning, and free WiFi.

4. Hotel Le Meridien: This chic, up-to-date five-star hotel is situated in the center of Buenos Aires and provides its guests with the finest in elegance and

comfort. The hotel offers a range of services and facilities, including an outdoor pool, a fitness center, and many dining choices. The hotel's rooms and suites include elegant design and modern conveniences including flat-screen Televisions, air conditioning, and free WiFi.

5. Sheraton Salta Hotel and Spa: The opulent five-star Sheraton Salta Hotel and Spa is situated in the center of Salta. The hotel offers a range of services and facilities, including an outdoor pool, a fitness center, and many dining choices. The hotel's rooms and suites include elegant design and modern conveniences including flat-screen Televisions, air conditioning, and free WiFi.

6. Loi Suites Recoleta: This opulent five-star hotel is situated in the center of Buenos Aires and provides its visitors with the ultimate luxury and leisure. The hotel offers a range of services and facilities, including an outdoor pool, a fitness center, and many dining choices. The hotel's rooms and suites include elegant design and

modern conveniences including flat-screen Televisions, air conditioning, and free WiFi.

7. NH Collection Buenos Aires Centro Historico: This elegant five-star hotel is situated in the center of Buenos Aires and provides its guests with the finest in comfort and elegance. The hotel offers a range of services and facilities, including an outdoor pool, a fitness center, and many dining choices. The hotel's rooms and suites include elegant design and modern conveniences including flat-screen Televisions, air conditioning, and free WiFi.

8. Hotel Faena: Situated in the center of Buenos Aires, Hotel Faena is a five-star luxury hotel. With a wide range of facilities and services, this hotel provides the finest in elegance and comfort for its visitors. The hotel's outdoor pool, fitness facility, and an array of eating choices are available to guests. The hotel's rooms and suites include elegant design and modern conveniences including flat-screen Televisions, air conditioning, and free WiFi.

9. Palacio Duhau Park Hyatt: This five-star luxury hotel is situated in the center of Buenos Aires and provides its guests with the ultimate comfort and elegance. The hotel offers a range of services and facilities, including an outdoor pool, a fitness center, and many dining choices. The hotel's rooms and suites include elegant design and modern conveniences including flat-screen Televisions, air conditioning, and free WiFi.

10. Intercontinental Buenos Aires: Situated in the city's center, Intercontinental Buenos Aires is a five-star luxury hotel. With a wide range of facilities and services, this hotel provides the finest in elegance and comfort for its visitors. The hotel's outdoor pool, fitness facility, and an array of eating choices are available to guests. The hotel's rooms and suites include elegant design and modern conveniences including flat-screen Televisions, air conditioning, and free WiFi.

SECTION FIVE

EATING AND DRINKING LIKE A LOCAL

Every food or beverage aficionado is likely to enjoy eating and drinking like a native of Argentina. There is something for everyone, from the classic asado (barbecue) to the renowned Argentine steak and wine.

For every culinary fan, the classic Argentine asado is a must-try. Meat is cooked in the asado method over an open flame. It is often served with sides like potatoes and chimichurri, a sauce consisting of herbs, garlic, and vinegar. Asado is a fantastic opportunity to experience the local cuisine and learn about the culture of the area.

Argentina is well-known for its top-notch meat, which is what makes its steak so delicious. The greatest cuts of steak are available at many of the local steakhouses along with a range of sides including chimichurri, mashed potatoes, and roasted veggies. The experience is equally as vital as the steak, even if it is the star of the show. It's a unique experience to eat in an Argentinian steakhouse, where you may take in the ambiance and the companionship of friends and family. Argentina is renowned for its wine as well. The most common grape in the nation, malbec, is used to make some of the finest wines in the whole world. Argentina's Malbecs are renowned for their strong, robust flavors, which make them the ideal match for steak or any other food. Try some of the regional wines produced in the Mendoza region's high-altitude vineyards for a one-of-a-kind experience.

It's an experience you won't soon forget to eat and drink like a native in Argentina. There is something for everyone to enjoy, from the classic asado to the renowned steak and wine of Argentina. So pour yourself a drink of Malbec, get ready for an asado feast, and prepare to taste the finest Argentinean cuisine.

The Best Places to Eat and Drink

Argentina is one of the greatest locations to get some of the most distinctive and delectable foods and beverages in the globe because of its reputation for producing top-notch food and beverages. The nation has plenty to offer for everyone, from age-old Argentine specialties to cutting-edge fusion cuisine. These are a few of Argentina's top locations for finding delicious food and beverages.

1. Parrillas: The traditional Argentinean grill restaurants, or parrillas, are among the greatest locations to discover succulent grilled meats, veggies, and fish. In addition to offering a broad selection of beers and wines, many parrillas are the ideal place to unwind with a delicious meal.

2. Street Food: The street food culture in Argentina is thriving, and many of the country's tastiest delicacies can be found there. Argentina has some of the greatest and

most reasonably priced street cuisines in the world, from empanadas to choripan.

3. Pizza: Pizza is a national dish of Argentina, and the nation is home to numerous top-notch pizzerias. Argentina has a wide variety of pizzas, including both traditional Margherita and inventive fusion varieties.

4. Argentina is famed for its superb tea and coffee, and the nation is home to a large number of cafés and tea shops. You may discover anything to sate your hunger for tea or coffee, from traditional Argentinian tea to one-of-a-kind mixes.

5. Wineries: Argentina is home to some of the world's top wineries, making it the ideal location to experience some of the greatest wines produced globally. It's a great place for wine enthusiasts since so many vineyards provide tours and wine samples.

6. Bars and Pubs: Argentina has a thriving and energetic bar and pub culture that is the ideal place to have a few

drinks and dance the night away. You may choose from authentic artisan beers to classic Argentinian beer to quench your thirst.

Restaurants: There are many different types of restaurants in Argentina, serving anything from fusion food to classic Argentinian fare. Argentina offers a variety of eating options, whether you're searching for a quick bite or a fine dining experience.

Argentina has much to offer for everyone, whether you're seeking classic Argentine recipes or something more distinctive. The greatest cuisine and beverages can be found in Argentina, from mouthwatering grilled meats to superb wines and specialty breweries.

Top Local Markets

Tourists and locals alike must visit Argentina because of its vibrant markets, which sell a wide range of regional items and vegetables. There are a variety of regional markets and bazaars that provide a unique shopping experience, from the crowded streets of Buenos Aires to the charming towns and villages in the countryside. The best marketplaces in Argentina are listed here for your convenience.

Marketplace in San Telmo

In the center of Buenos Aires, there is a lively market called Mercado de San Telmo. It is one of the city's oldest marketplaces and provides a variety of products, including antiques, handicrafts, souvenirs, and typical Argentine cuisine. A weekly antique fair is another aspect of the market, where you may discover some uncommon and distinctive items.

The market of the Abyss

The province of Santa Fe's capital, Rosario, is home to the Mercado de Abasto. With more than 150 kiosks offering everything from apparel and household goods to fresh food, it is the biggest market in Argentina. It's a terrific location to buy locally crafted crafts as well as fresh fruits and veggies.

Mataderos Festival

In the western region of Buenos Aires, there is an outdoor market called the Feria de Mataderos. Because it is held in a former cattle market, it is a bustling market with a classic vibe. Fresh foods, flowers, handicrafts, and authentic Argentine cuisine are all available here. The market is a terrific spot to explore traditional Argentine culture since it is also well-known for its folk music and dance.

The market of La Boca

In Buenos Aires' La Boca district lies the Mercado de La Boca, a vibrant market. It is a well-liked destination for both visitors and residents since it provides a variety of things, including fresh vegetables, apparel, accessories, and souvenirs. The market's brilliant colors make it a fantastic location for photography, and the bustling atmosphere will make your trip there one you won't soon forget.

Market of Recoleta

In Buenos Aires' Recoleta district sits the Mercado de Recoleta, a thriving market. It is one of the busiest markets in the city and sells a variety of products, including fresh produce, apparel, accessories, and souvenirs. It's a fantastic area to find some unusual products and take in the city's bustle.

These are just a few of Argentina's best marketplaces for you to check out. The nation provides a range of marketplaces and bazaars that give a unique shopping experience, from the busy streets of Buenos Aires to the charming towns and villages of the countryside. Argentina has something for everyone, whether you're seeking locally grown food, handcrafted goods, or trinkets.

SECTION SIX

OUTDOOR ADVENTURES

Argentina offers a broad variety of outdoor activities that will amaze and excite any explorer. Argentina is a delight for people who love the outdoors, with its majestic mountain ranges, lakes, rivers, and glaciers.

Argentina contains some of the highest peaks in the world for mountaineering. Argentina is home to Aconcagua, the tallest mountain in the Americas. Aconcagua is a fantastic spot to stretch your boundaries and put your talents to the test if you're up for the task. The breathtaking settings and breathtaking vistas combine for an experience you won't soon forget. The Andes, the Patagonia Ice Field, and the Monte Fitz Roy are other well-liked mountain ranges for climbers.

Argentina is a fantastic location for trekking and hiking. You may select a route to fit every level of expertise, from quick day walks to lengthy expeditions. To see the renowned Perito Moreno Glacier, visit Los Glaciares, National Park. One of the few glaciers in the world that is still expanding and moving toward a lake is this amazing glacier. Argentina has huge popularity for water sports. On the many rivers that traverse the nation, kayaking and rafting are popular activities. Although you may kayak through breathtaking canyons on the River Negro, the Rio Chico provides a more laid-back experience. Also popular on the Atlantic coast and the Iguazu River are windsurfing and kiteboarding.

Argentina provides a variety of bicycle routes for those who would rather remain on the land. There are many pathways to discover, whether you like road riding or mountain biking. To experience some of the greatest mountain ridings in the nation, go to the Quebrada de Humahuaca.

Last but not least, think about paragliding in Argentina for a unique experience. Paragliding is a fantastic method to gain a bird's eye perspective of the nation because of its stunning mountain ranges and vast open expanses. Try tandem paragliding with an expert instructor for an extra exceptional experience.

Argentina has much to offer no matter what your interests are in outdoor activities. It is the ideal location for an active holiday due to its beautiful surroundings and variety of activities.

Hiking

Argentina is a fantastic place to hike. Argentina provides a broad range of landscapes and paths to explore, from the breathtaking snow-capped Andes to the verdant Pampas. Argentina is a hiker's dream due to its extensive collection of natural treasures.

Argentina's Andes Mountains are home to some of the most breathtaking hiking. There are many different paths to explore in this mountain range, which is home to some of the highest peaks in the world. Hikers may choose a trail that fits their ability level and interests, from the well-traveled paths in the Patagonian area to the untamed mountain passes of the northern Andes.

Hikers can experience Argentina's verdant woodlands and grasslands in the Pampas area. In addition to having some of the most beautiful and interesting hiking routes in the nation, this area is home to some of the most biodiverse environments in the whole globe. Hikers may choose a path that matches their interests, from excursions along the Pampa River to treks into the subtropical rainforests of the Gran Chaco.

Another fantastic location for hikers is Argentina's northwest. There are many different routes to explore in this area, which has some of the most stunning vistas in the nation. Hikers may choose a path that fits their ability level and interests, from the arid desert trails of Salta Province to the lush highlands of Jujuy Province.

You can be sure that wherever you choose to trek in Argentina, you will be rewarded with breathtaking vistas, varied landscapes, and an abundance of species. Argentina boasts a range of hiking opportunities, from quick day hikes to larger multi-day treks. Get ready for an exciting journey in Argentina by donning your hiking boots!

Street Cycling

In Argentina, road cycling is a well-liked sport, and many of the finest riders in the world call Argentina home. It is a fantastic location for cyclists of all skill levels, providing a diversity of landscapes, difficult routes, and some of South America's most breathtaking scenery.

The Vuelta Ciclista Argentina, one of the most significant races in the area, is only one of the country's main road cycling competitions. It is a ten-day stage race that takes place every year in late March or early April and passes through some of Argentina's most breathtaking landscapes. While cyclists go over a variety of terrain, including steep mountain passes and rolling hills, during the Vuelta Ciclista, spectators get a fantastic chance to witness the finest of Argentina cycling.

Other significant events, like the Vuelta del Sol, the Vuelta del Sur, and the Ruta de los Conquistadores, are also held in Argentina. These competitions, which take place around the nation, are a wonderful opportunity to discover the variety of Argentina's scenery. The nation also has a great infrastructure for cycling on the highways, including well-maintained rural roads and designated bicycle lanes and trails spread across the cities.

While the weather in Argentina might vary greatly depending on the location, it is often moderate and favorable for riding. With its chilly climate and high heights, the Andes mountain region presents a special challenge to cyclists. Cycling in the Patagonia area may be challenging due to the region's harsh weather, which includes high winds and rain.

Generally speaking, cycling in Argentina is safe, although it's vital to use care while riding through cities and towns. Also, it is advised against riding at night since there is a larger danger of theft.

In general, Argentina is a fantastic travel destination for road cyclists, offering top-notch infrastructure, stunning scenery, and a range of difficult courses and competitions. Argentina will undoubtedly provide a unique experience, whether you are an expert rider or a novice.

Mountain biking

Argentina has seen a rise in the popularity of mountain biking in recent years as the nation has become a favorite destination for visitors who like an active lifestyle. For mountain bikers of all skill levels, Argentina provides a variety of difficult and fascinating courses thanks to its different landscapes and varied terrain. Mountain bikers may discover a range of paths and landscapes, each of which offers a distinctive experience, from the Andes peaks to the pampas and the Atlantic coast.

The Andes and the Pampas are the two primary mountain biking areas in Argentina. With its challenging, technical routes, untamed landscape, and breathtaking vistas, the Andes area is home to some of the greatest mountain riding in the whole globe. The Pampas area offers a more leisurely journey because of its undulating hills, grasslands, and woodlands. For riders of all ability levels, both locations provide a range of trails, from challenging single-track to wide-open double-track.

The number of mountain biking trails and bike parks has increased in Argentina as a result of the sport's popularity. There are several beginner to expert-level routes in the Andes, but a few of the more well-known ones include the El Condor Trail in San Rafael, the Mendoza Trail System, and the Ruta de los Volcanes in Patagonia. The San Luis Trail, the La Pampa Trail, and the La Estancia Trail are three of the most well-traveled paths in the Pampas.

In addition to the routes, Argentina has a variety of bike parks where riders may improve their abilities and enjoy the landscape. The most well-known parks are the Los Alerces Bike Park in Bariloche, the La Pampa Bike Park in La Pampa, and the La Estancia Bike Park in La Estancia. Riders may test their abilities and explore the terrain in all of these parks, which provide a variety of beginner to difficult routes and attractions.

Argentina's different landscapes may be explored and the local culture can be fully appreciated through mountain riding there. Argentina is a paradise for mountain cyclists of all skill levels because of its diverse terrain, breathtaking vistas, and bike parks. Argentina has something for everyone, whether you're searching for a relaxed ride or a difficult challenge. So why not explore Argentina's trails and bike parks if you're searching for adventure?

Skiing

For many fans of winter sports, skiing in Argentina is an amazing experience. Argentina has some of the top ski areas in the world, making for an incredible skiing experience.

The Andes mountain range, which crosses Argentina from south to north, is where the ski resorts are situated. The provinces of Mendoza, San Juan, Rio Negro, Neuquén, Chubut, and Santa Cruz, as well as other regions of the nation, all have several ski resorts. The ideal months to visit the resorts are July and August, while the ski season runs from June through October.

Argentina's ski resorts are renowned for having exceptional snow and slopes, as well as a diversity of terrain that is appropriate for skiers of all skill levels. In addition to restaurants, pubs, stores, ski lifts, ski lodges, and ski schools, the resorts provide a variety of facilities. Several resorts now provide ski packages that include lodging, lift tickets, ski equipment rentals, and instruction.

Las Leas, which is situated in the province of Mendoza, is one of the most well-known ski areas in Argentina. With a vertical drop of more than 1,500 meters and an extensive ski area covering more than 500 hectares, this resort is renowned for its exceptional snow conditions. The World Cup Skiing Championships have been held at Las Leas, which provides a variety of activities for skiers of all skill levels.

Cerro Catedral, a well-liked ski resort in Argentina, is situated in the Rio Negro region. This resort has a variety of sports, including snowmobile, snowshoeing, and tubing, as well as a large number of ski lines for skiers of all skill levels. Moreover, Cerro Catedral provides a range of ski packages that include lodging, lift tickets, and ski equipment rental.

You will have an outstanding time at whichever ski resort you select in Argentina. Argentina is a terrific place to go skiing because of its stunning landscape, top-notch ski routes, and top-notch amenities.

Snowboarding

Argentina's snowboarding industry is one of the most well-known winter sports in the nation. The geography of the nation is diverse, ranging from the calm Andean foothills to the treacherous, steep mountains of the Patagonian area.

The ski resort of Las Leas, which is situated in the Andes highlands, is the most well-liked snowboarding location in Argentina. The snowboarding at Las Leas is among the finest in the world, and there is a vast range of terrain available for all skill levels. There are two major ski areas in the resort, one for novices and the other for more experienced skiers. The ski area also has a sizable halfpipe and a terrain park for freestyle skiers.

Cerro Castor, which is situated in the Patagonian area, is another well-liked snowboarding location in Argentina. From novice to advanced riders, Cerro Castor has a variety of terrain to offer. In addition, the resort has a sizable terrain park, a superpipe, and several other amenities. Argentina has year-round opportunities for snowboarding, with the greatest snow often occurring during the winter. Nonetheless, summer is the greatest season to go since the slopes are less crowded and the weather is more comfortable.

Overall, snowboarding in Argentina is a fantastic chance to experience some of the greatest snowboarding in the world while seeing the nation's varied terrain. Everyone may find something to appreciate, whether they like the calm Andean slopes or the difficult landscape of the Patagonian area.

kayaking, rafting, and boating

Argentina is a stunning, multicultural nation famous for its amazing mountains, glaciers, and rivers. In this South American nation, boating, kayaking, and rafting are common pastimes that provide tourists the opportunity to take in breathtaking landscapes and distinctive animals.

Argentina's many lakes, rivers, and canals are perfect for exploring by boat. The Parana River, the largest and most significant river in the nation, is the ideal location for a relaxing boat trip. Little islands, abundant animals, and beautiful flora border the river's banks. The Parana provides access to the Uruguay, Paraguay, and Iguazu rivers. In addition, a variety of fauna, such as dolphins, alligators, and enormous anteaters, call these rivers home. Visitors may tour tiny towns and villages along the road and discover the history and culture of the area.

A fantastic way to discover Argentina's varied landscapes is via kayaking. Argentina's kayaking opportunities range from serene lakes and rivers to the Andes Mountains' whitewater rapids, so there is something for everyone. Although the violent rapids of the Rio Grande are excellent for more seasoned kayakers, the waters of the Iguazu River are great for novices. Kayaking in Argentina is a fantastic way to see the native animals, including caimans and capybaras. Rafting is a fantastic way to discover Argentina's rivers. With its hard rapids and breathtaking landscape, the Rio Grande is a well-known rafting destination. In addition to providing breathtaking views of the Andes Mountains and the chance to see animals like caimans and capybaras, the Upper Parana is a fantastic alternative for rafting. Rafters may also take in the spectacular scenery of the Iguazu Falls by exploring the Iguazu River.

Visitors may explore Argentina's breathtaking landscapes and take in the country's distinctive fauna by boat, kayak, or raft. These activities provide a fantastic opportunity to see the beauty of Argentina, from the serene lakes and rivers to the violent rapids of the Andes Mountains. Argentina has plenty to offer everyone, whether you're an expert paddler, kayaker, rafter, or novice eager to try something new.

Nightlife

For visitors seeking to enjoy its thriving nightlife, Argentina is a distinctive and interesting location. Argentina's nightlife has something for everyone, from the classic tango bars and clubs of Buenos Aires to the salsa and reggae bars of the north. Argentina provides something for everyone, whether they are searching for a quiet evening or a crazy night out.

The nightlife in Buenos Aires is active and varied. Traditional tango bars and contemporary techno clubs are only a few of the bars and clubs that are available to suit diverse interests. While there are many more areas to discover, the majority of pubs and clubs are located in the hip neighborhoods of Palermo and Recoleta. The city is bustling with music and street entertainers throughout the day. As the sun goes down, the city becomes a lively and exciting place to be. Every tourist in Buenos Aires should visit one of the city's authentic tango bars. Live music, passionate dancers, and delectable food and beverages can all be found at these pubs. Visit one of the city's numerous techno clubs for a more contemporary experience; these establishments provide a special fusion of music, dancing, and beverages.

Argentina's nightlife changes as you go farther north. The nightlife is more laid-back and loose in the northern provinces of Salta, Jujuy, and Tucuman. There are many native foods and beverages available here, as well as pubs and clubs playing salsa and reggae music. These pubs and clubs have a considerably more laid-back vibe than those in the city's center, making them the ideal place to spend a night out with friends.

You'll find a terrific night out in Argentina wherever you choose to go. Argentina's nightlife offers something for everyone, from the classic tango bars and clubs of Buenos Aires to the salsa and reggae bars of the north. Argentina offers everything you might want, whether you're searching for a quiet evening or a crazy night out.

Festivals and events

Argentina is a multicultural and energetic nation with a culture that is firmly established in its past and customs.

Argentina has several festivals and events that honor the history and traditions of the country, ranging from traditional folk festivals to concerts of contemporary music. Visitors may expect a range of experiences due to the distinctive traditions and festivals that are exclusive to each area of the nation.

In Argentina, Carnival, which takes place in late February or early March, is the most significant holiday. Parades, music, and dancing are all part of this joyous festival. People participate in several dances while wearing vibrant, colorful costumes during the Carnival celebrations. It is a season of pleasure and celebration and a wonderful chance to get to know the people and culture of Argentina. Every year in March, Mendoza hosts the Fiesta Nacional de la Vendimia (National Grape Harvest Festival). This event honors the region's wine and grape-growing industry. The event offers tours of nearby vineyards along with music, dancing, and cuisine. Visitors may engage in several events and contests as well.

La Rioja hosts the Fiesta Nacional del Sol (National Sun Festival) in January or February. This event features singing, dancing, and drinking as ways of honoring the sun. Traditional practices like bullfighting and rodeo contests are also highlighted. Guests may take pleasure in the festival's lively atmosphere as well as the traditional foods and beverages that are supplied.

In May, Catamarca hosts the Feria de la Plata (Silver Fair). With a variety of events including parades, music, and dancing, this is a celebration of the area's silver output. There are various contests, such as beauty pageants and cuisine competitions. Together with participating in traditional dances, tourists may eat and drink locally.

Every April, Buenos Aires hosts the Fiesta Nacional de la Cerveza (National Beer Festival). With a range of events including beer tastings, music, and dancing, this is a celebration of the country's beer culture. Visitors may take part in tournaments and other events as well.

Guests may also take pleasure in the festival's traditional cuisine and beverages.

There are other additional festivals and events held throughout the year in Argentina. They include the National Apple Festival (Fiesta Nacional de la Manzana), National Flower Festival (Fiesta Nacional de las Flores), and National Fishermen's Festival (Fiesta Nacional de los Pescadores). Visitors get the chance to explore the culture and customs of the country during each of these events.

In Argentina, there is always something to appreciate, no matter what time of year it is. In this dynamic and varied nation, there is something for everyone to enjoy, from traditional folk festivals to performances of contemporary music.

Month by month

January

In Argentina, January marks the beginning of the year and is a festive month. The cold to moderate temperatures is ideal for outdoor activities. It's an ideal time to travel since the sun is out and the days are long. Warm temperatures and a lush, green environment may be found towards the north. The snow-covered Andes mountains in the south provide breathtaking vistas and skiing chances. Tierra del Fuego and Iguazu Falls are two of Argentina's numerous national parks that are fantastic to visit in January.

February

In Argentina, February is a fantastic month for sightseeing. It's the perfect time to explore the nation since the weather is still moderate and the days are long. The northern hemisphere has temperate to warm temperatures and a rich vegetated environment. The snow-covered Andes mountains in the south provide breathtaking vistas and skiing chances. The month of February is also a fantastic time to go to Buenos Aires. There are several cultural occasions, such as the Tango Festival and La Boca Carnival.

March

Argentina's spring season begins in March when temperatures range from moderate to warm. It's a terrific time to go since the days are longer. The northern hemisphere has temperate to warm temperatures and a rich vegetated environment. The snow-covered Andes mountains in the south provide breathtaking vistas and skiing chances. With its numerous cultural events and festivals, March is a fantastic time to visit Buenos Aires.

April

Argentina is a wonderful place to visit in April since the days are long and the weather is pleasant to warm. The northern hemisphere has temperate to warm temperatures and a rich vegetated environment. The snow-covered Andes mountains in the south provide breathtaking vistas and skiing chances. An excellent month to visit Buenos Aires is April because of all the festivals and cultural events that take place there.

May

Argentina is a wonderful place to visit in May since the days are long and the weather is pleasant to warm. The northern hemisphere has temperate to warm temperatures and a rich vegetated environment. The snow-covered Andes mountains in the south provide breathtaking vistas and skiing chances. The Fiesta de la Primavera and the Buenos Aires International Film Festival bring life to the city of Buenos Aires in May.

June

Argentina is a wonderful place to visit in June since the days are long and the weather is pleasant to warm. The northern hemisphere has temperate to warm temperatures and a rich vegetated environment. The snow-covered Andes mountains in the south provide breathtaking vistas and skiing chances. With its many cultural events and festivals, like the Festival de la Diversidad Cultural, June is a fantastic time to visit Buenos Aires.

July

Argentina is a wonderful place to visit in July since the days are long and the weather is pleasant to warm. The northern hemisphere has temperate to warm temperatures and a rich vegetated environment. The snow-covered Andes mountains in the south provide breathtaking vistas and skiing chances. The month of July is a wonderful time to visit Buenos Aires because of all the festivals and cultural events that take place there, including the Fiesta de la Independencia.

August

Argentina is a wonderful place to visit in August since the days are long and the weather is pleasant to warm. The northern hemisphere has temperate to warm temperatures and a rich vegetated environment. The snow-covered Andes mountains in the south provide breathtaking vistas and skiing chances. With its numerous cultural events and festivals, like the Festival de la Culture, August is also an excellent month to visit Buenos Aires.

September

Argentina is a wonderful place to visit in September since the days are long and the weather is pleasant to warm. The northern hemisphere has temperate to warm temperatures and a rich vegetated environment. The snow-covered Andes mountains in the south provide breathtaking vistas and skiing chances. The Festival de Teatro and other cultural festivals, as well as the city of

Buenos Aires' numerous other activities, make September a fantastic month to visit.

October

Argentina is a wonderful place to visit in October since the days are long and the weather is pleasant to warm. The northern hemisphere has temperate to warm temperatures and a rich vegetated environment. The snow-covered Andes mountains in the south provide breathtaking vistas and skiing chances. Buenos Aires hosts a variety of cultural events and festivals during October, including the Festival de la Msica.

November

Argentina is a wonderful place to visit in November since the days are long and the weather is pleasant to warm. The northern hemisphere has temperate to warm temperatures and a rich vegetated environment. The snow-covered Andes mountains in the south provide breathtaking vistas and skiing chances. The Festival de la Ciencia and other cultural celebrations, as well as the city of Buenos Aires itself, make November a fantastic month to visit.

December

Argentina is a wonderful place to visit in December since the days are long and the weather is pleasant to warm. The northern hemisphere has temperate to warm temperatures and a rich vegetated environment. The snow-covered Andes mountains in the south provide breathtaking vistas and skiing chances. The Festival de la Navidad and other cultural celebrations, which take place in December, make it a perfect time to visit Buenos Aires.

Information and Services

One of the biggest nations in South America, Argentina provides its residents with a vast array of information and services. The nation offers access to a range of services, from communication and transportation to healthcare and education.

Both governmental and private organizations provide healthcare in Argentina. Government funding supports the public healthcare system, which offers all residents universal coverage. Private healthcare is also accessible to individuals who can afford it thanks to government subsidies. The public healthcare system is well-established and offers a variety of services, such as primary care and preventative care. Argentina places a high importance on education. Up to the secondary level, free public education is offered. Also, the government offers financial aid to people who want to pursue higher education. Moreover, there are other private colleges and universities around the nation that provide a wide range of programs.

In Argentina, radio, television, and the internet are the major forms of communication. Many radio stations and television networks throughout the nation deliver news, entertainment, and instructional content. Email, online browsing, and social networking are just a few of the things that people do on the internet, which are readily accessible.

The road system in Argentina is primarily responsible for providing transportation. Major cities are connected by a multitude of highways and roads across the nation. In most cities, there are also public transit options, such as buses, trains, and subways. Many areas of the nation are serviced by the national rail network.

Argentina is a sizable, diversified nation that offers a broad variety of products and services. The nation offers access to a range of services, from communication and transportation to healthcare and education. Argentina is a popular tourism and immigration destination due to its robust economy and well-developed infrastructure.

Argentina with Children

Argentina is a dynamic and disregarded South American nation that provides tourists with a wide range of locations and family-friendly activities. Argentina offers something for everyone, even kids, from the vibrant city of Buenos Aires and Rosario to the unspoiled, natural marvels of Patagonia and Tierra del Fuego.

Argentina has a variety of attractions and activities for families with kids, including anything from outdoor recreation to cultural encounters. Families may visit the historical sites and thriving cultural areas of the capital city of Buenos Aires. The city also provides a variety of fun things to do for kids, such as parks, zoos, and aquariums. All ages may take advantage of Buenos Aires' energetic nightlife, which offers a variety of family-friendly restaurants, cafés, and pubs.

Iguazu Falls, one of the most breathtaking natural wonders on earth, are located in Argentina's north. Children may go up close to the falls by wandering along the pathways and taking in the sights from boat cruises, which will mesmerize them with their thunderous roar. Kids may engage in a variety of activities in the neighborhood, including swimming in the pools and exploring the local forest and nature trails.

Patagonia is a breathtaking area located in the southernmost part of Argentina. You may explore the breathtaking scenery, enormous glaciers, and varied fauna here with your kids. Children may engage in a variety of activities around Patagonia, such as horseback riding, kayaking, and hiking. Children may also enjoy boat cruises to visit the nearby islands and experience the wild terrain of Tierra del Fuego.

From the exciting city of Buenos Aires and Rosario to the breathtaking natural marvels of Patagonia and Tierra del Fuego, Argentina offers a variety of unique experiences for kids. Argentina is the perfect vacation spot for families with kids because of its variety of animals, activities, and culture.

Regions at a Glance

Argentina is a sizable nation with a diverse climate and significant natural beauty. It is situated in the southern region of South America, and Chile, Bolivia, Paraguay, and Uruguay are its neighbors. Argentina is made up of 23 provinces plus Buenos Aires, the country's capital, which is an independent city. Districts and departments are further separated into provinces.

The Pampas, the Andes, the Cuyo, and Patagonia are the four different geographic areas that makeup Argentina. Every area has a distinct climate, topography, and culture of its own.

The Pampas

One of the biggest and most significant agricultural areas in the world is the Pampas region in Argentina. It is situated in the country's central-east and extends from the Atlantic Ocean in the east to the Andes Mountains in the west, covering an area of around 720,000 square kilometers.

The flat terrain, mild temperature, and rich soil of the Pampas area are its defining features. This makes it the perfect location for farming and rearing cattle. The region's primary economic activity is agriculture, and the Pampas are thought to contribute to more than half of Argentina's total agricultural output. There are several minor villages and cities in the area as well, which provide locals with job possibilities.

The Pampas area is perfect for cultivating a range of commodities, including cereals, vegetables, fruits, and olives due to its rich soil and temperate environment. Wheat, barley, maize, and soybeans are the principal crops farmed in the area. The region's economy also heavily relies on the production of livestock, with sheep and cattle being the most significant types of animals.

Several of Argentina's most recognizable and well-known sights, including the Iguazu Falls, the Perito Moreno Glacier, and the Pampas grasslands, are located in the Pampas area. Moreover, it is home to some of the most significant archaeological sites in the world, including the remains of the Inca capital of Cusco.

The Pampas area is a well-liked travel destination, providing tourists with a range of activities including horseback riding, hiking, and bird-watching. Several national parks, including the Parque Nacional de los Glaciares and the Park Nacional de las Sierras de Cordoba, are also located in this area.

The Pampas region has a variety of cultural influences, including both European and indigenous civilizations. The local cuisine, which is renowned for its use of regional ingredients and conventional cooking techniques, reflects this.

The Pampas area is a significant contributor to Argentina's economy and culture and provides tourists with a distinctive and diverse experience. The Pampas area is a memorable travel destination because of its breathtaking scenery and dynamic culture.

The Andes

Argentina's Andes area, which spans the whole of the nation's western side, is a very diversified and distinctive terrain. The Andes mountain range, which spans Argentina's north to south, is what makes up this area and is where many of the country's most recognizable landscapes can be found. With its lofty peaks, vast canyons, luxuriant woods, and majestic rivers, it is a place of extraordinary beauty and majesty.

Several of Argentina's tallest peaks are located in the Andes, which are the world's longest mountain ranges. At 6,960 meters above sea level, Aconcagua is the second-highest peak in the world and the highest mountain in Argentina. At a height of 6,739 meters, Cerro Bonete is the second-highest summit in the nation. Several additional noteworthy summits may be found in the Andes, such as the 6,539-meter Cerro de los Aleros and the 6,152-meter Cerro de los Gigantes.

Several of Argentina's most beautiful national parks are located in the Andes. One of Argentina's most well-known parks, El Glaciares National Park is home to some of the most breathtaking glaciers on earth. The Perito Moreno glacier, one of the most popular tourist destinations in the nation, is located near Los Glaciares. Another outstanding national park in the Andes is Parque Nacional Nahuel Huapi. Many glaciers, rivers, and lakes, as well as some of the nation's most untamed and breathtaking peaks, may be found in this protected region.

Many unusual animals and plants may be found in Argentina's Andes. Pumas, jaguars, spectacled bears, llamas, and other diverse animals may be found in the Andes. The area is also home to several bird species, including hummingbirds, condors, and Andean geese. The quinoa plant, for example, is found in the high-altitude regions of the Andes and is one of the many plants that call the mountains home.

Argentina's Andes area is a stunningly varied and gorgeous region that is home to some of the nation's most magnificent fauna and scenery. The Andes is an incredible experience and a must-visit location for anybody wishing to discover the magnificence of Argentina, from the highest mountain peaks to the deepest gorges.

The Cuyo

The provinces of Mendoza, San Juan, and San Luis make up Argentina's Cuyo area, which is situated in the country's central-western corner. The provinces of La Rioja and Catamarca, La Pampa and Buenos Aires, Neuquén, and Ro Negro form its northern, eastern, and southern borders, respectively. The Andes Mountains, the Cuyo Desert, and the Pampas Grasslands are just a few of the area's stunning natural features.

With several pre-Colombian archaeological sites, the Cuyo area is rich in history and culture. The Huarpe people and the Incas were the earliest inhabitants of the area, and the Incas left their imprint with the Inca Trail, a network of roads and trails that linked the many communities in the area. In the 16th century, the Spanish occupied the area, and many of its towns still have colonial architecture today.

The Cuyo area is well-known for its wine production, which has long played a significant role in the local economy. More than 200 wineries can be found in the area, which also produces some of the greatest wines in the world, including the well-known Malbec.

The Cuyo area is also well-known for its natural wonders, including San Juan's stunning Laguna del Diamante and the highest mountain in the western hemisphere, Aconcagua Mountain. Together with the scenic lakes of Caviahue and Villarrica, the Copahue hot springs is another attraction for tourists in the area.

The Cuyo area is renowned for having a thriving nightlife with a wide variety of taverns and clubs. Many celebrations and events are also held in the area, including the yearly Feria del Vino wine festival in Mendoza.

The Cuyo area is a well-liked tourist destination because of its breathtaking natural beauty, bustling nightlife, and rich culture. It is understandable why the Cuyo area of Argentina is one of the most well-liked travel destinations in South America given its wealth of attractions.

The Patagonia

Argentina's Patagonia region, which spans the southernmost point of South America, is a vast, rocky, and sparsely inhabited territory. Patagonia is a region in Argentina's southern half that runs from the Atlantic Ocean in the east to the Andes Mountains in the west as well as from the River Colorado in the north to the Strait of Magellan in the south. It is one of the most secluded and lonely areas on the continent, and it has unrivaled natural beauty.

Wide steppes, green plains, deep fjords, snow-capped mountains, massive glaciers, and deserts are just a few of Patagonia's spectacular scenery. The many national parks, nature preserves, and other natural places that are accessible to tourists let visitors see this varied landscape.

A wide variety of animals and birds, including guanacos, foxes, deer, pumas, condors, and other species, may be found in the area. For discovery and adventure, whether it be hiking, camping, mountain biking, or kayaking, its large open areas are ideal. In addition, there are several museums and archaeological sites that provide light on the history and culture of the area.

Some of Argentina's most exquisite and opulent resorts may be found in Patagonia. These resorts offer guests a variety of services, such as spa services, golf courses, excellent cuisine, and local region excursions. In addition, the resorts provide access to a range of outdoor activities including horseback riding, fishing, and climbing.

Argentina's Patagonia area is a special vacation spot with plenty to offer everyone. Patagonia is the perfect location for people wishing to discover and enjoy the best of Argentina, with its spectacular natural beauty, an abundance of animals, luxury resorts, and outdoor activities. Argentina is a multicultural nation with a distinct culture. Travelers may encounter a variety of things in its four areas, including the beautiful Andes, the sweeping Pampas, and wild Patagonia. Every area has its unique personality, which makes it a wonderful destination for every tourist.

SECTION EIGHT

PLANNING YOUR TRIP

A fascinating journey, planning a vacation to Argentina may include a wide range of activities. Planning a vacation to Argentina may be enjoyable and fulfilling, whether your goal is to visit the lively cities, breathtaking natural marvels, or rich cultural legacy of the nation. Here are some suggestions for organizing your vacation to Argentina:

1. Choose Your Destination: From the magnificent Iguazu Falls to the vibrant Buenos Aires, Argentina has a lot to offer. Choose the destinations and activities you wish to participate in while organizing your vacation. Take into account the size of the nation and the length of time you have.

2. Examine the Weather: The climate in Argentina varies greatly from area to region. Although the south is often

colder and more humid, the northern portion is normally warm all year round. Before you go, check the weather so you can pack appropriately.

3. Take Safety into Account: Traveling to Argentina is typically safe, but it's necessary to be aware of your surroundings and exercise basic safety measures. It's wise to keep your belongings handy and to avoid wandering alone at night in some of the bigger cities.

4. Reserve Accommodations: Argentina offers a range of lodging choices, from hostels to five-star hotels. To guarantee you receive the greatest deal, research hotels in the region you're intending to visit and make your reservations early.

5. Money Exchange: The Argentine peso is the country's unit of currency. As exchange rates in Argentina may not be as beneficial as those in other nations, it is preferable to convert money before traveling.

6. Get a Visa: Before visiting Argentina, you may be required to do so, depending on your place of origin. Before you go, research the visa requirements and submit applications for the required paperwork.

7. Pack Suitably: Be sure to include clothes and other things that are suitable for the environment and the activities you'll be participating in. Consider the weather while choosing your clothing.

Organizing a vacation to Argentina may be enjoyable and thrilling. You can make your vacation unique and pleasurable with some careful study and preparation.

Itineraries

One of the most exciting experiences one may have is a trip to Argentina. Argentina is a beautiful nation with a rich culture and history. This stunning South American nation has something for everyone, from the vibrant capital of Buenos Aires to the magnificent Iguazu Falls.

It is crucial to have a well-considered itinerary while arranging a vacation to Argentina. The cities of Buenos Aires, Cordoba, and Mendoza should all be included in a normal itinerary for a vacation to Argentina.

Day 1: Buenos Aires

Start your journey in Buenos Aires, the capital and most populous city of Argentina. There are many things to do in this dynamic city, which is rich in culture and history. Explore the city all day, from the Plaza de Mayo to the well-known La Boca area. Spend some time exploring the city's museums and art galleries while also indulging in some of its delectable food.

Day 2: Cordoba

Leave Buenos Aires and go to the city of Cordoba. The Jesuit Block and Estancias de Cordoba are two remarkable colonial-style structures in this city. See the adjacent Jesuit Missions, which were named UNESCO

World Heritage Sites in 2000, after spending the day visiting the city.

Day 3: Mendoza

Make your journey to Mendoza, a city famous for producing wine. The greatest wines from the area may be tasted while spending the day visiting the vineyards. Spend some time exploring the stunning Andes Mountains in the adjacent Aconcagua Provincial Park.

Day 4: Iguazu Falls

Iguazu Falls should be the last stop on your tour to Argentina. You won't want to miss seeing this magnificent natural marvel, which is one of the most breathtaking sites on the planet. Spend some time exploring the national park, which has miles of rainforest and hundreds of waterfalls.

You will never run out of intriguing things to do in Argentina, regardless of how long you want to stay there.

You won't be disappointed with your vacation, whether you spend time discovering the vibrant cities or marveling at the stunning waterfalls. You can ensure that you enjoy the most of what Argentina has to offer by planning your trip carefully.

The best time to visit

There is no one-size-fits-all solution to the issue of when is the ideal time to visit Argentina since it is a huge and varied nation. The optimal time to travel may vary greatly depending on the sort of traveler you are, the season, and the location you are visiting.

The ideal time to come is between December and February if you want to take advantage of the country's natural beauty and enjoy a range of outdoor activities. The hottest months in the nation are December, January, and February, which are ideal for outdoor activities.

The greatest season to enjoy skiing and snowboarding in the Andes is from June to August, while the best time to explore the Patagonian and Lake Region of the nation is from March to May. While it might be fairly windy, the temperature is pleasant during this time.

The ideal time to come if you want to experience the culture is between March and May. This is a perfect time to enjoy the local festivities and culture of the nation since many of them, including the Fiesta de Mayo, take place then. Travelers should also take advantage of the lower pricing and fewer people during the shoulder seasons of April and October. These months are ideal for seeing the nation's many attractions since the weather is relatively moderate.

Lastly, due to the warm, bright weather, the summer months of December to February are the busiest for travel. Nonetheless, the cost and the crowds may also be oppressive.

In general, there is no right time of year to visit Argentina that applies to everyone. The ideal time to travel may vary greatly depending on the sort of traveler you are and the location you are visiting.

What to Pack

If you're planning a trip to Argentina, you should carefully examine the weather, the activities you'll be doing, and any special cultural traditions that may apply. Your packing list should be customized to your schedule since Argentina is a huge nation with a variety of weather and varied regions, each with its special traditions.

Clothing

* Lightweight clothes for warm weather: For Argentina's warmer climes, cotton T-shirts, shorts, and skirts are all excellent choices. A light jacket should be brought along just in case it becomes chilly at night.

* Layering clothing for milder climates: In mountainous areas, the temperature may drop significantly at night. To

be warm, bring layers like a light jacket, a sweater, and a long-sleeved shirt.

* Footwear: While touring Argentina, you must wear comfortable shoes. Carry along a pair of flip-flops or sandals for the beach as well as a pair of sneakers or walking shoes.

* Swimwear: Pack your swimwear if you want to visit the beach or go swimming.

* Accessorize: Sunglasses, a hat, and a scarf may all keep you warm in colder areas and shield you from the sun.

* Cultural attire: Depending on your schedule, you may wish to include more conventional attire like a poncho or gaucho hat.

Essentials

Remember to bring your personal belongings, including a toothbrush, toothpaste, deodorant, and any necessary prescriptions.

* Electronics: Be careful to include the correct adapters and chargers if you want to use your devices in Argentina.

* Cash: It's possible that certain locations in Argentina won't take credit cards, so be sure to pack plenty.

* Paperwork: Passport, visa, and any other necessary crucial papers.

* Travel Insurance: In the event of any unforeseen circumstances, having travel insurance is usually a smart idea.

* Toiletries: Don't forget to bring any additional amenities you may need, such as shampoo, conditioner, soap, and sunscreen.

* Snacks/Drinks: Bring some snacks and energy drinks if you anticipate spending a lot of time on the go.

Here are a few of the necessities to bring for your trip to Argentina. Remember to have fun and make sure to adjust your packing list to reflect your specific plan.

Travel Insurance

Each journey, particularly one to Argentina, should take travel insurance into account. It might be easier to guarantee that your vacation will be safe and pleasant if you have appropriate coverage for medical charges and other unforeseen costs.

Argentina is a well-liked tourist destination because of its stunning landscape and dynamic culture. But, it's crucial to keep in mind that this South American nation is also prone to several natural calamities, such as earthquakes and harsh weather. It's crucial to get travel insurance that can protect you in case of an emergency since medical treatment in Argentina may also be pricey.

The kind of coverage you need should be taken into account while searching for a travel insurance policy for Argentina. Basic coverage for medical costs, lost or stolen property, and trip cancellation or interruption will often be included in insurance. Nonetheless, you have to likewise hunt for supplemental insurance that can safeguard you in case of an emergency.

When you need to be evacuated to a hospital in another nation, for instance, some insurance includes coverage for emergency medical evacuation. Consider legal aid insurance as well, which might be useful if you run into any legal issues while visiting Argentina.

And last, a lot of insurance covers adventurous sports and endeavors like skiing, bungee jumping, and scuba diving. If you want to engage in any of these activities while visiting Argentina, be sure your insurance is sufficient.

No of the kind of travel insurance coverage you choose, be sure to thoroughly read the tiny print before making a purchase. This will guarantee that you are fully aware of both the policy's inclusions and exclusions. You may go to Argentina in safety and comfort if you have the appropriate insurance.

Documentation and visa requirements

Travelers who want to visit Argentina must meet stringent visa and documentation requirements. Argentina is a well-liked tourism destination. The restrictions may change depending on whether the trip is being taken for business, tourism, or another reason. The papers and visa requirements for travel to Argentina are shown below.

Visa:

Visitors from a few countries may get an Argentina visa upon arrival. These nations include the majority of those in Europe as well as the United States, Canada, Australia, and New Zealand. Visa applications must be made in advance for nationals of nations that are ineligible for visas on arrival. A valid passport, two passport-style pictures, proof of a return flight, proof of lodging, and evidence of adequate cash for the length of the stay are required to apply for a visa.

Documentation:

Travelers visiting Argentina will also need to show additional documentation at the border in addition to a current visa. This includes having a current passport that is still valid at least six months after the anticipated travel date. Together with a valid return ticket, travelers must provide evidence of having enough money to last the length of their trip. A hotel reservation or a letter of invitation from a host in Argentina may be required as additional documentation for tourists. Visitors must be aware that a business visa is necessary if they are going on business. Candidates must provide a current passport, proof of a return flight, and evidence of adequate cash to cover the period of the stay to be considered for a business visa. A letter of invitation from the company in Argentina is also required, as is documentation demonstrating the applicant's professional skills and expertise for the intended purpose of the visit.

Lastly, entry into Argentina may require passengers to provide evidence of immunizations or health insurance. Entry into the nation is not subject to vaccination requirements, although visitors entering from a nation where yellow fever is an issue may need to provide documentation of a current yellow fever vaccine. Also, it is advised that visitors obtain full-coverage health insurance to pay for any medical costs incurred while in Argentina.

In conclusion, visitors to Argentina must have a current visa and appropriate papers to enter the nation.

Depending on the objective of the trip, different regulations may apply, therefore it's important to make sure all paperwork is in order before leaving.

How to Purchase Tickets

There are several alternatives open to you if you need to purchase tickets for an Argentine vacation. You may be able to get tickets from several sites, depending on your location and spending limit.

You may research conventional travel agencies, internet travel agencies, and airlines directly to find out about airfare. Travel brokers may be able to provide specials or packages that might help you save money. If you're prepared to wait until the perfect time to book, online travel agencies may also offer specials or discounts and sometimes lower pricing. Several airlines provide flights to Argentina, so you may compare costs and itineraries to get the ideal one for your vacation.

If you need to buy rail tickets, you may do it immediately at the train station or online at websites. Tickets for both domestic and international rail travel are widely available online. You may also inquire about discounts and special deals at the railway station.

You may buy bus tickets online or at the bus station if you're planning to travel by bus. Bus tickets are widely available online for both local and international routes. Also, if you make a reservation in advance, certain bus operators could offer offers or discounts. You may buy boat tickets directly from the boat business or online through websites. Tickets for both local and international boat trips are widely available online. Also, if you make a reservation in advance, certain boat operators could offer offers or discounts.

Last but not least, if you need tickets for any other mode of transportation, such as taxis or auto rentals, you may get them directly from the businesses or through internet services. Several online travel agencies sell tickets for various modes of transportation.

There are several resources available to assist you in finding the tickets you need for your Argentina vacation, regardless of the kind of tickets you are searching for. You can get the greatest bargains and reduce the cost of your vacation by doing some research and comparing costs.

COST

Depending on the kind of vacation you're doing and how long you spend there, going to Argentina might be pricey. Argentina is renowned for being more affordable than other nations in South America, but travel expenses may mount up fast.

Argentina air travel may be expensive, particularly during the summer. Aeroparque Jorge Newbery, the primary hub for international flights, is Argentina's principal airport and is situated in Buenos Aires. A round-trip ticket may cost anywhere between $500 and $1,500 depending on where you are traveling from, with prices rising during holidays and during high travel times.

Depending on where you stay and the sort of hotel you choose, Argentina's lodging options might be rather varied. Hotels in Buenos Aires are available in a variety of price ranges, from $50 to $200 for a single night. The cost of a bed in a dorm room at a hostel, on the other hand, maybe an excellent choice for travelers on a tight budget, with rates beginning at around $15 per night. Airbnb is another option, however, costs might be expensive owing to the significant demand from visitors from outside.

Depending on the kind of meal you like, eating out in Argentina might also be pricey. Supper at a neighborhood eatery or on the street may cost as little as $10. But, costs might be fairly exorbitant if you're seeking more sophisticated eateries. In a midrange restaurant, supper for two may run you around $50.

Long-distance travel in Argentina may be fairly expensive in terms of transportation. Domestic flights may cost between $100 and $200, although bus and rail tickets only cost around $30. Taxis are another choice, but they can be quite pricey, with single-ride costs ranging from $10 to $30.

Last but not least, when traveling to Argentina, it's critical to consider the cost of activities and attractions. The cost of visiting well-known tourist destinations like the Andean Lakes, the Perito Moreno Glacier, and the Iguazu Falls are generally quite high. These attractions can charge $20 to $100 for admission.

Overall, depending on your itinerary and the kind of trip you're taking, the cost of visiting Argentina can vary significantly. Argentina is renowned for being more affordable than other nations in South America, but travel expenses may mount up fast. To make your trip as affordable as possible, it's critical to budget and plans ahead.

SECTION NINE

SAFETY AND SECURITY

Argentina is a South American nation renowned for its stunning landscapes, illustrious culture, and energetic cities. The nation is a dream location for vacationers, with everything from the snow-capped Andes Alps to the sweltering jungles of the Amazon. Nonetheless, there are several safety considerations and safeguards that visitors should be aware of in order to guarantee a safe and secure stay.

The first and most crucial safety precaution is to always be aware of your surroundings. Pickpockets and other small-time crooks are active in tourist locations, so it's crucial to be cautious with your possessions and avoid carrying a lot of cash. Avoiding solo travel is also a good idea, particularly at night.

Getting travel insurance before you go is the next safety precaution. This may be quite helpful in an emergency and will cover any medical expenses you may have while in Argentina.

Avoid utilizing unauthorized "pirate" cabs and always employ trustworthy taxi firms when it comes to transportation. Also, as there have been instances of ticket fraud in the past, it is advised to purchase airline and rail tickets from trusted companies.

It's crucial to be mindful of the local animals while traveling in rural regions. Despite the fact that Argentina is home to some of the most stunning wildlife in the world, it's crucial to keep in mind that some of these creatures may be harmful. While dealing with wild animals, it is best to exercise caution and heed the recommendations of local guides.

Lastly, it's critical to understand the nation's political climate. While there have been occasional episodes of civil turmoil in the past, Argentina is typically a secure country. It is essential to avoid any sizable gatherings and to be aware of any potential protests or demonstrations. Argentina is a stunning, energetic nation with a lot to offer. Travelers may guarantee a secure and pleasurable trip by adhering to these safety and security precautions.

Health and Safety

Argentina is a stunning nation with a dynamic culture and breathtaking scenery. It is also the second-largest nation in South America, which often encourages a big number of tourists to visit the nation to take in its numerous attractions. Argentina is a beautiful country, but it's not always the safest to go there. The nation's high rates of crime, poverty, and health concerns are well-known.

It is crucial to be aware of the hazards and take preventative measures when it comes to safety. Visitors should use additional caution while traveling in some regions of the nation since they are more hazardous than others. Visitors should be very alert of their surroundings since theft, robbery, and abduction are widespread in several places. Also, it's crucial to stay away from crowded areas and protests.

There are various possible concerns to take into account in terms of health. Diseases including typhoid, cholera, and hepatitis may be brought on by contaminated water. By avoiding ice cubes and consuming bottled water, many illnesses may be avoided. Visitors should take measures like using mosquito nets and bug repellent since malaria is also prevalent in certain locations. Argentina's poor air quality may contribute to respiratory conditions including bronchitis and asthma. Visitors should put on a face mask while outside in very polluted places to help protect themselves from this. Moreover, vaccinations against diseases including rabies, yellow fever, hepatitis A and B are advised.

Despite the dangers, if the proper measures are followed, Argentina is a fantastic and safe location to go. Always be aware of your surroundings and take the essential safety precautions while visiting. They may do this without being concerned about their health or safety, allowing them to take in the country's beauty and culture.

Medication and Vaccinations

Vaccinations and drugs play a significant role in the public health system in Argentina. The spread of many infectious diseases may be stopped by vaccinations, which also act as a barrier against possible ailments. Many diseases may be prevented using vaccines, which are often given out free of charge by the public health system.

The National Immunization Program (NIP) in Argentina offers vaccinations to both children and adults. The National Institute of Vaccines and Serums and the Ministry of Health collaborated on the initiative. Polio, diphtheria, tetanus, hepatitis B, and influenza are just a few of the diseases that are protected against by the program. Typically, vaccinations are administered in two doses, the first at birth and the second at age five. The program also offers booster dosages to make sure people continue to have the required level of immunity.

In addition to immunizations, pharmaceuticals play a significant role in Argentina's public health system. In addition to HIV/AIDS and viral disorders, medications are available for a wide range of conditions, including cancer, cardiovascular problems, diabetes, and cancer. The public health system often offers medications free of charge. Medicines may sometimes be covered by private insurance policies or by government subsidies. By the implementation of universal health care, the Argentinean government has taken action to increase access to pharmaceuticals. This includes programs like the National Drug Plan, which offers pharmaceuticals at a reduced cost to those who are 18 years of age or older and offers financial aid to people who cannot pay the full cost of prescriptions. The government has also made measures to improve access to pharmaceuticals in rural regions, such as expanding the number of pharmacies and offering financial aid to those who need prescriptions but cannot pay them.

In general, Argentina's government has taken action to guarantee that people have access to the immunizations and treatments they need. Free vaccinations are offered, and either government subsidies or deeply reduced costs are available for prescription drugs. These programs have aided in enhancing public health in Argentina and halting the spread of infectious illnesses.

What to do in case of Emergency

It is crucial to maintain composure and take the appropriate action in the event of an emergency in Argentina. There are certain actions that must be followed to safeguard your safety and the safety of others, depending on the situation.

The best thing to do in case of a medical emergency is to call 107, the emergency hotline. The National Medical Emergency System (SAME), which is accessible to the general public around-the-clock, may be reached at this number. When you call the number, the operator will inquire about your location and the emergency's specifics. In order to get the best answer, it's critical to offer precise information. An ambulance may be sent to the site in specific circumstances.

It is crucial to stay indoors and adhere to local authorities' directions when faced with a natural catastrophe, such as a flood or earthquake. The neighborhood police will often provide advice and support. It is crucial to avoid any locations that have been affected by the tragedy and to only leave the house if the authorities tell you to.

The best thing to do in the case of a fire is to leave the structure as soon as it is safe to do so. It is crucial to use the stairs rather than the elevators. When leaving the building, it's crucial to keep a safe distance from it while you wait for the fire department to come.

It is crucial to call the police if you have been the victim of a crime. 911 should be called in case of emergency in Argentina. In order to guarantee that the culprit is apprehended, it is crucial to supply as much information as you can. Also, it's crucial to keep your composure and refrain from challenging the offender.

Lastly, it's crucial to get in touch with your country's embassy if you need help while visiting Argentina. The Embassy will often be able to provide guidance and support in an emergency.

In general, it's crucial to maintain your composure and heed local authorities' directions in the event of an emergency in Argentina. In order to protect your safety and the safety of others, it is also crucial to get in touch with the appropriate emergency services as soon as you can.

SECTION TEN

SURVIVAL GUIDE

Custom Regulations

Many customs laws that are implemented by the Argentine Customs Agency apply to visitors to Argentina (Aduana Argentina). To guarantee a comfortable and trouble-free vacation, it is crucial to be aware of these rules.

All visitors to Argentina are required to disclose their cash, jewelry, and other valuables when they arrive. All cash above $10,000, as well as jewelry and other valuables, must be disclosed. Also, a thorough inventory of the objects being declared may be required by customs officers. It is significant to remember that Argentina strictly prohibits the importation of any potentially harmful items, including firearms, explosives, military hardware, and other items.

Tourists are permitted to import several commodities, including cigarettes, wine, and fragrances, as long as they fall within the predetermined restrictions when it comes to duty-free goods. For instance, guests are permitted to bring in up to 50 milliliters of perfume, two packs of cigarettes, or 200 grams of tobacco in addition to up to two liters of wine or liquor. Anything that is purchased for more than these sums will be regarded as importation and be subject to taxes and customs.

Moreover, visitors are permitted to carry some things into the country for their use, including clothes, literature, and small appliances. Unfortunately, these products cannot be marketed in Argentina and must only be used for personal use.

It is also crucial to remember that any products brought into the nation must be disclosed upon arrival. Visitors run the danger of having their belongings seized by customs officers if they fail to declare them.

Moreover, travelers should be aware that Argentina's import policies are subject to change at any time and without prior warning. To be sure that the most recent rules are being followed, it is usually preferable to verify with the Argentine Customs Agency before departing.

Discount cards

Tourist discount cards in Argentina provide a wide range of reductions and advantages. These cards may be used to get discounts on activities, lodging, meals, purchases, and travel. These cards are intended to make discovering Argentina's rich cultural diversity, stunning natural surroundings, and energetic cities simpler and cheaper.

The Turista Plus card and the Descuentos Touristcard Argentina are the two most widely used discount travel cards in Argentina. Discounts are available with cards for eating, shopping, lodging, and activities. Although the Descuentos Touristcard Argentina gives savings on vehicle rentals and airport transfers, the Turista Plus card also offers discounts on transportation.

A prepaid card called the Turista Plus card offers savings of up to 50% at restaurants, hotels, and activities. Moreover, it provides savings on modes of transportation including cabs, metro lines, and buses. The card may be acquired online or in tourist information offices, and its validity is up to a year. A prepaid card called the Descuentos Tourist Card Argentina offers savings of up to 20% at restaurants, hotels, and attractions. Also, it provides savings for public transit, airport transfers, and vehicle rentals. The card may be acquired online or in tourist information offices, and its validity is up to a year.

Both cards are excellent choices for tourists seeking to save costs on their trip to Argentina. They provide reductions on a variety of tourist attractions, lodging, eating, shopping, and transportation. These are a fantastic alternative for anyone planning long trips in Argentina since they are simple to use and are good for up to a year.

Tourists in Argentina may save money by using discount cards while they travel the nation. Discounts are offered on tourist attractions, lodging, eating, shopping, and transportation. These are a fantastic alternative for anyone planning long trips in Argentina since they are simple to use and are good for up to a year.

Electricities

Argentina is a South American nation that is quickly rising to prominence in the electrical industry. With a total installed capacity of more than 39,000 megawatts, the nation has the most energy available in South America. A combination of hydroelectric, nuclear, and thermal power facilities provide Argentina's energy.

With more than 50% of the country's total capacity, hydroelectricity is the main source of power in Argentina. The Yacyreta Dam, which is situated on the Parana River in the northern region of the nation, is the biggest hydroelectric infrastructure there is. This project, the second-largest hydroelectric plant in the world, has a total generating capacity of 3,380 megawatts. The Salto Grande Dam, with a capacity of 1,630 megawatts, and the Piedra del Aguila Dam, with a capacity of 1,060 megawatts, are two other significant hydroelectric facilities in the nation. At almost 20% of the total capacity, nuclear power is Argentina's second-largest source of energy. Atucha I, Atucha II, and Embalse are the three nuclear power stations in the nation. The combined capacity of the three, which are all in the province of Buenos Aires, is 3,375 megawatts. The government-owned Nucleoelectrica Argentina company runs each of these facilities.

With almost 30% of the total capacity, thermal power ranks third among sources of energy in Argentina. While some are powered by diesel or coal, natural gas is the primary fuel for the majority of the nation's thermal power plants. The Azul-Tandil facility, which is situated in the province of Buenos Aires, is the biggest thermal power plant in the nation. The state-owned energy corporation YPF owns and operates this facility, which has a 2,200-megawatt capacity overall.

Argentina is likewise spending a lot of money on alternative energy sources. By 2025, the nation wants to produce 20% of its power from renewable sources. To do this, the government has put in place a variety of laws and programs that encourage the growth of renewable energy sources including wind, solar, and biomass. To cut down on its use of power, the nation is also investing in smart grid technology and energy efficiency.

Overall, Argentina is developing rapidly in the electrical industry and is headed toward taking a significant leadership position in the world power market. The nation uses a variety of electrical generation methods and is heavily investing in energy-saving and renewable technology. With these investments, Argentina is in a good position to take the lead in the future of the electrical industry.

Internet Access

In Argentina, access to the internet is often quick and dependable. More than 17.7 million individuals in the nation have access to the internet, with a penetration rate of 68.8%. In comparison to other Latin American nations, this represents a high level of internet availability.

The Argentinean government has taken several steps to increase internet access there. The government introduced "Plan Vive Digital" in 2009, which gave residents in rural regions free internet connection. More than 6 million individuals have successfully connected to the internet thanks to the strategy. To ensure that every person has access to high-speed internet by 2020, the government also made investments in enhancing the broadband infrastructure.

DSL is the most popular kind of internet connectivity in Argentina. Most of the major telecom providers in the nation provide this. There is also cable internet service accessible, although it is more costly and less common. Due to the availability of 4G LTE networks in the majority of the country's main cities, mobile internet access is also growing in popularity.

Internet connectivity is quite inexpensive in Argentina. In comparison to cable and mobile internet, DSL connections generally cost $20 to $40 per month. The monthly cost of high-speed internet subscriptions may reach $50.

Argentina typically has an adequate internet connection overall. The nation has worked to increase rural residents access to the internet, and the service is reasonably priced. To guarantee that every person has access to the internet, however, there is still more work to be done.

Opening Hours

The majority of establishments, shops, and restaurants in Argentina have rather rigid opening hours. Although some retailers may stay open late, most businesses shut their doors around 8 p.m. and it's likely they don't reopen until the next day. The majority of shops and businesses are typically closed on Sundays as a day of relaxation.

From Monday through Saturday, the majority of businesses and malls in Argentina are open at 10 a.m. and shut at 8 p.m. On weekdays, banks are typically open from 10am to 5pm, however, some locations could shut earlier on Fridays. Sundays and Saturdays are often off days for banks.

Argentina's grocery shops typically are open from 9am to 8 p.m. on weekdays and from 10 a.m. to 7 p.m. on Saturdays. On weekdays, certain shops may remain open until 9 p.m. and on Saturdays, until 8pm On Sundays, grocery shops are closed.

In Argentina, pharmacies typically open at 8 a.m. and shut at 10 p.m. On weekdays and Saturdays, certain pharmacies may remain open longer, while many shut sooner on Sundays.

The hours of operation for restaurants in Argentina vary. For lunch, most restaurants open at noon and shut at 3 p.m.; for dinner, they open again at 8 p.m. and close at 11 p.m. On Fridays and Saturdays, certain eateries may remain open later.

On weekdays, public transit in Argentina typically operates from 5 a.m. to 1 a.m., while on weekends and holidays, it operates from 6 a.m. to 12 a.m.

In general, Argentina's business hours are different from those in other nations. Compared to other nations, the majority of retailers and restaurants shut early, and many are closed on Sundays. While traveling in Argentina, it's crucial to make advance plans since certain establishments may not be open when you expect them to.

Public Holidays

1. New Year's Day (1 January): Argentina observes New Year's Day as a national holiday.

2. Epiphany (6 January): Often referred to as the Day of the Three Kings, Epiphany is a national holiday in Argentina and is observed on that day.

3. Carnival (February/March): Argentina observes Carnival as a public holiday on the Tuesday before Ash Wednesday.

4. Good Friday (March/April): Argentina observes Good Friday as a public holiday in March or April.

5. May Revolution (25 May): The May Revolution, often referred to as the Day of the First National Government, is observed on May 25 and is a national holiday in Argentina.

6. Independence Day (9 July): Argentina observes Independence Day as a national holiday on the ninth of July.

7. National Flag Day (20 June): Argentina observes National Flag Day as a public holiday on 20 June.

8. National Day (20 August): Argentina observes National Day as a public holiday on 20 August.

9. Columbus Day (12 October): In Argentina, Columbus Day is observed as a public holiday on that day.

10. All Saints' Day (1 November): In Argentina, All Saints' Day is observed as a public holiday on November 1.

11. Immaculate Conception (8 December): In Argentina, the 8th of December is a national holiday honoring the Immaculate Conception.

12. Christmas Day (December 25): In Argentina, Christmas Day is observed on that day and is a national holiday.

CONCLUSION

As you can see, Argentina is a nation with a lot to offer, including its beautiful landscapes, energetic cities, rich cultural legacy, and varied animals. Argentina has plenty to offer everyone, whether they are seeking a once-in-a-lifetime trip or a memorable cultural encounter. Argentina is a place that will leave you with lifelong memories, from the vivacious culture and fantastic nightlife of Buenos Aires to the beautiful Andes Mountain peaks. Argentina has much to offer everyone with its welcoming people, varied food, and interesting attractions. So why not go about and take in everything that this lovely nation has to offer? You won't be sorry.

Printed in Great Britain
by Amazon

19989937R00098